Brilliant Activities to

Stimulate Creative Thinking

Stretch Gifted and Talented Children – and Everyone Else – in Primary Schools

Will Hussey

Brilliant
PUBLICATIONS

We hope you enjoy using this book. If you would like further information on other titles published by Brilliant Publications, please write to the address given below or look on our website: www.brilliantpublications.co.uk.

Written by Will Hussey

Where Can an Elephant Roost? Challenges to Ignite Learning at Key Stage 2
Where Can an Elephant Hide? Challenges to Ignite Learning at Key Stage 1

Written by Ashley McCabe Mowat

Brilliant Activities for Gifted and Talented Children
Brilliant Activities for Stretching Gifted and Talented Children
CRAMES – Creative Games to Help Children Learn to Think and Problem Solve (in only 5 minutes a day!)

Thinking Strategies series

Thinking Strategies for the Successful Classroom, 5–7 Year Olds
Thinking Strategies for the Successful Classroom, 7–9 Year Olds
Thinking Strategies for the Successful Classroom, 9–11 Year Old

Published by Brilliant Publications
Unit 10
Sparrow Hall Farm
Edlesborough
Dunstable
Bedfordshire
LU6 2ES, UK

E-mail: info@brilliantpublications.co.uk
Website: www.brilliantpublications.co.uk

The name Brilliant Publications and the logo are registered trademarks.

Written by Will Hussey
Illustrated by Chantal Kees

Contents

Introduction

These activities are most definitely not for everyone. If you are the sort of person who likes a straightforward 'yes-or-no' question, then perhaps you should read no further. Still here? Then hopefully there's more to you than meets the eye (just kidding).

Brilliant Activities to Stimulate Creative Thinking delivers something a bit special; a fun cerebral workout that reaches parts of the brain that ordinary everyday considerations generally do not. It provides a wealth of varied and thought-provoking activities that encourage the reader to contemplate the gaps between the familiar. By entertaining new possibilities and exploring alternative perspectives, children enjoy expressing the riches of their imagination. **Brilliant Activities to Stimulate Creative Thinking** is designed to help children reach their Personal Best, and exercise their full potential.

The book consists of five broadly overlapping ' brain workouts':

Brain gain	**Quick draw**	**Movers and shakers**	**Create and make**	**Chicken and egg**

Each workout contains a wide variety of exercises that stimulate readers to think creatively and encourages children to explore different ways of expressing new ideas more clearly. Those familiar with Bloom's Taxonomy will recognize that **Brilliant Activities to Stimulate Creative Thinking** facilitates the three higher order levels of thinking skills: analysis, synthesis and evaluation.

- **Analysis** necessitates understanding the attributes of something so that the component parts may be studied separately and in relation to one another. Asking pupils to compare and contrast, categorize and/or recognize inference, opinions and motives helps to develop analytical thinking.

- **Synthesis** requires children to create a novel or original thought, idea or product. All the activities we call 'creative thinking' give pupils experience with synthesis. Also, when pupils take bits and pieces of several theories or combine ideas from different sources to create an original perspective or idea, they are thinking at a synthesis level.

- **Evaluation** encourages children to judge and consider their analysis. Utilizing these three capabilities helps to ensure children are fully challenged, meeting the needs of those identified as gifted and talented. A categorical list of the activities is available at the back of the book.

Thinking differently, thinking again and thinking one-step-ahead require mental agility and the capacity to 'dig deeper'. Without such attributes, development is limited to a superficial understanding. **Brain gain challenges** (analysis and evaluation) sustain concentration, encouraging focus for longer periods in the quest to make sense. By creating just the right amount of dissonance, children become acclimatized to the feeling of deciphering, and increase their thought-processing stamina.

Of course for some of us 'seeing is believing'. The ability to visualize a particular concept or scenario can help to clarify understanding: bringing the relevant parameters in to sharper conscious focus. **Quick draw activities** (synthesis and analysis) develop this association by first prompting, then realizing, suggested mental pictures – extracting the 'image' from 'imagination'. They help the reader to literally draw their own conclusions.

Life on the whole is a collaborative experience for most. Interacting with others helps us to explore and further our understanding. Effectively sharing and responding to the ideas and opinions of others is essential for meaningful communication. **Movers and shakers challenges** (evaluation, analysis and synthesis) provide the food for collaborative thought – cultivating the skills necessary for accessing shared wisdom.

Whilst thoughts often translate in to action, conversely action can inform thinking. **Create and make activities** (evaluation and synthesis) are designed to lift ideas off the page, encouraging children to derive three-dimensional solutions and adjust their rationale in the process. By exploring 'hands on' possibilities, thinkers inform theoretical supposition with practical realization.

Chicken and egg challenges (analysis, synthesis and evaluation) embrace the old adage about there being 'more questions than answers'. Generating responses to some of those imponderables encourages children to think creatively as well as carefully. Progress can result from the ability to embrace a new perspective – responding unconventionally to the conventional. Chicken and egg challenges breed the confidence to think differently, and celebrate thought-provoking solutions.

In addition to these challenges, interspersed throughout the book is a little extra **Food for thought.** These tasks require the reader to decipher a variety of encoded dishes, some more familiar than others. These side orders provide a light alternative to the main course; something to chew over for a while before returning to the workout.

Brilliant Activities to Stimulate Creative Thinking recognizes that exercise should be fun. These brain workouts encourage creative ideas, independent thinking and originality. The activities foster a healthy interest in an alternative view of life – helping children to think for themselves and develop their own perspective. With a healthy mind, **Brilliant Activities to Stimulate Creative Thinking** gives children the confidence to rise to a challenge.

Getting started

Parents and teachers know that children are naturally active; given the choice, most things are completed at speed. Ask two children to cross the park and it will inevitably develop into some sort of race. The park swings seemingly defy gravity as one friend seeks to outdo the other. A pebble thrown in to the sea often results in a competition to find who can skim it furthest. Even when children are by themselves, there appears to be an innate temptation to test limitations; gauging whether something can be done faster, higher or stronger. They don't need a prescriptive training plan to keep active.

Brilliant Activities to Stimulate Creative Thinking works in a similar way: children will exercise their imaginations by simply visiting the playground of challenges. Some may prefer a particular type of brain workout, whilst others are keen to diversify; children enjoy pursuing existing interests or exploring new lines of enquiry. Children may decide to dabble in **Brilliant Activities to Stimulate Creative Thinking**, regularly returning to continue with their explorations for five minutes here and there. Alternatively they can become absorbed in a particular task, choosing to continue their train of thought towards a natural conclusion; either way works.

There are no hard and fast rules about undertaking the activities; children are simply encouraged to enjoy them and respond to them, as they feel appropriate. Whilst the nature of the tasks are clear, it is okay to develop a line of thinking at a tangent, or even in a contrary direction to initially intended.

Brilliant Activities to Stimulate Creative Thinking plants a seed of thought and cultivates ideas to grow and blossom. By engaging children with thought provoking ideas and encouraging them to respond in a variety of ways, they exercise individual potential.

Thanks to Ashley McCabe Mowat for her ideas in **Brilliant Activities for Stretching Gifted and Talented Children**.

Love notion

Just what do you mean by 'love'? Love can be
many different things to different people: maybe
a person, place, song, object, memory or even a
favourite food.

Write down your own ideas about how 'love' can
show itself.

Stimulate Creative Thinking

Under where?

You could take this challenge literally and think
about the things we all know are underfoot:
sewage pipes and foundations, for instance. Or
maybe, 'underground' could mean something a
little more subversive.

Draw a picture to illustrate your ideas.

Stimulate Creative Thinking

Words worth?

Politicians are renowned for saying something relatively simple in a long-winded manner.

Try to explain something straightforward to a friend in such a complicated way that it sounds quite the opposite. Can they work out what you're actually saying?

Sign language

We've all seen signs warning intruders to 'beware of the dog', but just how effective are they?

Construct an original sign warning uninvited visitors of an alternative encounter.

Quality street?

There are some road names that we like the sound of and some that we don't.

Make a list of all the street names you can think of where you would be happy to live. Explain why.

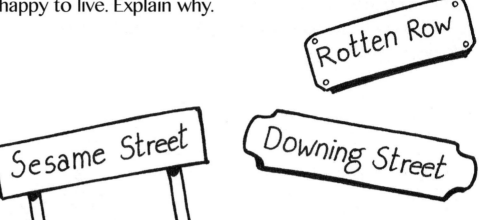

Stimulate Creative Thinking
© Will Hussey and Brilliant Publications

Cry maybe?

We're not just talking about onions here. It could be in a good way or a bad way, but what sorts of things bring a tear to your eye (even if you're the strong silent type)?

Draw ten teardrops and record something that would make you cry inside each one.

Stimulate Creative Thinking
© Will Hussey and Brilliant Publications

The dark night

The thought of some things can keep you awake at night: perhaps a particular experience not to be repeated or an irrational fear.

Draw a picture of whatever has you reaching for the light switch!

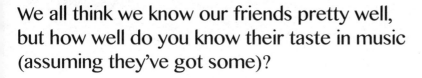

Thy tunes

We all think we know our friends pretty well, but how well do you know their taste in music (assuming they've got some)?

Write a list of songs that you think they would listen to, and then see what their reaction is. Can you justify your choices?

Colditz

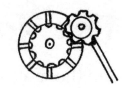

No one likes catching a cold, but imagine you could trap it and then get rid of it.

Design and build a 'cold catcher'. What does it look like and how does it work?

Stimulate Creative Thinking
© Will Hussey and Brilliant Publications

Shady characters

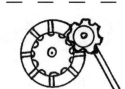

Some say that a colour is different to a shade. Does that mean that a door shaded aquamarine has no colour? Hmm...

Apply all the different colours and shades that you can think of to create pieces of a 'kaleidoscope' jigsaw.

Stimulate Creative Thinking
© Will Hussey and Brilliant Publications

Goodwill withdrawal

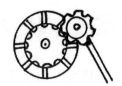

Cheques are used to transfer money between bank accounts, enabling customers to withdraw the value when convenient.

Design and make your own alternative 'cheque book' substituting sums of money for good deeds that you can undertake for friends and family.

11-1-89

I will put bins out

£

Fish eye Q

Tropical fish are a variety of colours, shapes and sizes and can look somewhat fantastical as a result.

Can you design an 'original' fish that is unique? Where has your inspiration come from?

Back draft

Sometimes you can be adamant that you are right, only later to realize that you were actually wrong.

Try to clearly relate one such instance to a friend. How did it make you feel and what did you do about it (if anything)?

Stimulate Creative Thinking
© Will Hussey and Brilliant Publications

Pupil progress

Do you have an eye for detail?

Construct a suitably realistic looking eyeball to view the surroundings. Find a place to position it to 'keep an eye on things'.

Stimulate Creative Thinking
© Will Hussey and Brilliant Publications

Score draw

Some popular books have subsequently been adapted into films.

How many different examples can you think of? You can include comic-book stories if you wish. Many of the blockbuster releases around these days have been based upon a book of some sort.

Bother nation

There are some days when everything seems to run smoothly and others when nothing feels like it's going to plan. Events conspire to make even the most straightforward of tasks more difficult than they should be.

Create a scenario when everything that could go wrong does; how are you and the people around you adversely affected?

Pic-as-ya

They say 'a picture speaks a thousand words'. Imagine someone could capture a snapshot that represents your interests, likes, dislikes and the people and places that are important to you.

Sketch a scene that captures the 'essence of you'.

Stimulate Creative Thinking
© Will Hussey and Brilliant Publications

Vision express

Some people profess to know what they want to do with the rest of their lives from a relatively young age. Other people take a completely different path to their initial interest and, of course, there are those who just don't have a clue!

Make a list of your friends on one piece of paper and on another devise a list of future occupations that you think would be fitting. Ask someone if they can successfully match the people with your suggested professions.

Stimulate Creative Thinking
© Will Hussey and Brilliant Publications

Dream engine

Dreams can be very illusive; some are more memorable than others. They can sometimes be explained by the events of the preceding day, or alternatively seem quite random.

Design and create a device for catching and analysing a dream. What different components would it need and how would they work?

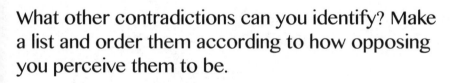

Blanc looks

White wine is sometimes described as being 'dry', yet the liquid itself is obviously wet. This description could be described as somewhat of a contradiction in terms.

What other contradictions can you identify? Make a list and order them according to how opposing you perceive them to be.

Hidden meanings

People who achieve spectacular results are sometimes said to be in possession of a 'box of tricks' to assist them. The actual contents often remain a mystery.

Devise the ultimate box of tricks. Decide what you would keep inside it and how the items might be put to good use.

Stimulate Creative Thinking
© Will Hussey and Brilliant Publications

Well heeled

'Designer' shoes are extremely expensive and can be much sought after. Not everyone thinks that they're worth it.

Design an alternative designer shoe, which you think would be genuinely valuable. Consider what materials you might use and any special qualities you could incorporate.

Stimulate Creative Thinking
© Will Hussey and Brilliant Publications

Food for thought

Can you crack the code to work out what's on the menu?

Main courses

Side dishes/snacks

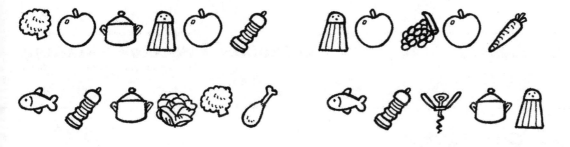

Desserts

In formed

There are some people that you meet most days, yet seemingly know relatively little about them.

Imagine a lifestyle for someone you know little about: consider his/her hobbies, interests and preferences. If you get an appropriate opportunity, share your observations, and see if there are any 'real-life' similarities.

Stimulate Creative Thinking
© Will Hussey and Brilliant Publications

Scream engine

No one likes a nightmare (shudder), but most of us have experienced one at some time or other.

Create a device for catching and analysing a nightmare. What particular components would it need and how would they work? Remember to keep yourself safe!

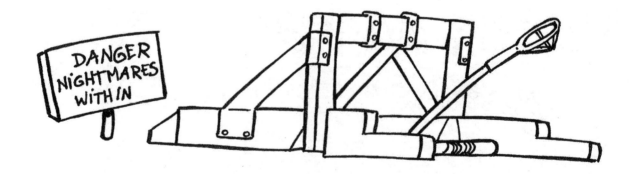

DANGER NIGHTMARES WITHIN

Stimulate Creative Thinking
© Will Hussey and Brilliant Publications

Smoke signals

Years ago, smoking was actually thought to be good for your health. Of course we now know this is not the case.

Consider what 'modern day' advice might be discredited in years to come. Describe any potential symptoms or side effects that might be caused. For example, bananas actually cause loneliness: you will lose 'a-peel' after a while!

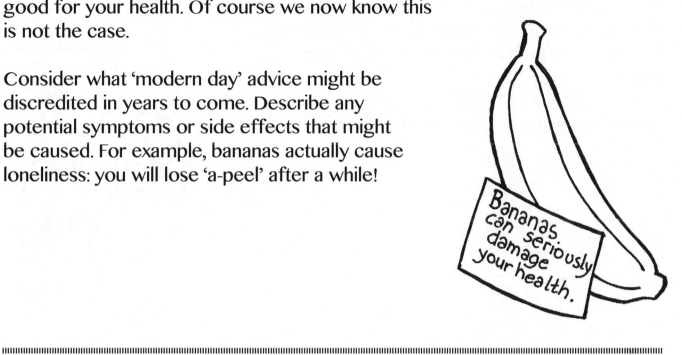

Bananas can seriously damage your health.

Know admittance

Some organizations or clubs have particular rules to which their members must adhere. If someone is found to break the rules they might be banned from participating – or become 'blacklisted'.

Who can you think of that might be blacklisted: where from and why?

No Admittance

Negative vibes

Imagine a photograph that represents your interests, likes, dislikes and the people and places that are important to you. Perhaps somewhere, someone a little like you has a very different picture.

Draw a snapshot of your life in a 'parallel universe'.

Stimulate Creative Thinking
© Will Hussey and Brilliant Publications

It takes two, baby...

Sometimes you can say it better with music...

Work with a friend to devise a 'conversation' consisting entirely of lyrics from songs that you can recall. Try to think of appropriate lines to continue the dialogue for as long as you can.

Stimulate Creative Thinking
© Will Hussey and Brilliant Publications

Time piece

For centuries people have dreamed about being able to travel forwards and backwards through time and space.

Imagine you have the blueprints for a device that will enable you to go where and when you want – into the future or rewind the past. Make your design into a three-dimensional reality!

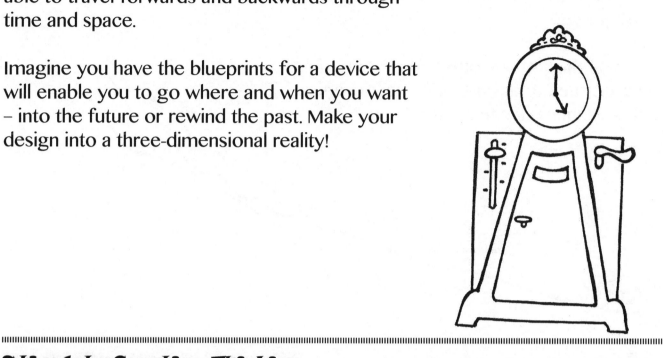

Wordly goods?

Words can evoke strong emotions and responses. Some words in particular have the power to shock and offend people.

There are other words, however, that maybe sound 'rude' but actually are not. How many examples of 'non-swear' words can you think of, and what do they really mean?

Seismic shift?

A 'kitchen-roll' is typically found in a kitchen, or alternatively could describe a consequence of an earthquake.

Can you think of any other items that could be construed to describe different events, circumstances or situations?

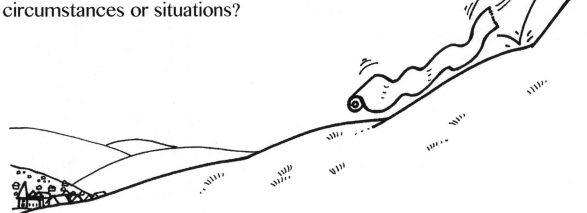

Stimulate Creative Thinking
© Will Hussey and Brilliant Publications

I can icon?

The symbols on a computer screen indicating the various different programs installed are referred to as 'icons'.

Some of the icons are more interesting than others. Can you design a 'new and improved' icon for a particular programme that you have used?

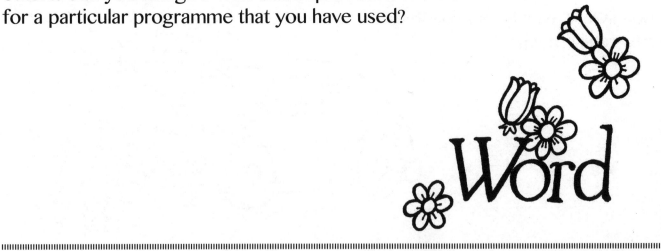

Stimulate Creative Thinking
© Will Hussey and Brilliant Publications

New order

You may think you know all there is to know about your friends and family.... But do you?

Converse with people close to you and try to find out a hitherto unknown piece of information. What do you consider to be the most significant revelation?

Action station

A person who is particularly keen to become involved in a situation or activity might be described as wanting 'a piece of the action'.

Create a sculpture that is inspired by this phrase.

Reader's digest

Some people prefer Italian food, others Indian or perhaps Cantonese. There is a varied selection of food available, originating from many different countries around the world.

Choose your favourite food 'genre'. List how many different dishes you can think of that would fall in to your chosen category.

For example, Italian food: spaghetti bolognaise, lasagne, pizza...

Stimulate Creative Thinking
© Will Hussey and Brilliant Publications

Tell me why?

Is it true that many people just don't like Mondays?

Explain why you think Monday is sometimes described as the most unpopular day of the week. How many creative ways can you think of for changing this?

Stimulate Creative Thinking
© Will Hussey and Brilliant Publications

Globe jotting

The earth is usually described as being comprised of seven large land masses or continents. How many of these can you name?

Sketch a map of the world solely from memory, before comparing it with the real thing. How accurate did you manage to be?

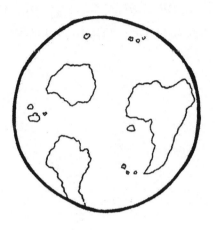

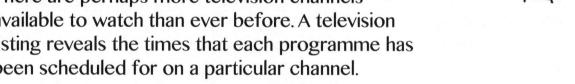

Televised debate

There are perhaps more television channels available to watch than ever before. A television listing reveals the times that each programme has been scheduled for on a particular channel.

Cooperate with a friend to try to devise a complete television schedule for a particular channel.

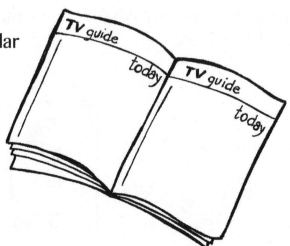

Card bored?

Mobile phones usually contain a Subscriber Identification Module – better known as a SIM card. This is a device that stores important data such as phone numbers and messages.

Examine an existing SIM card and then try and construct a replica. How authentic can you make it?

Stimulate Creative Thinking
© Will Hussey and Brilliant Publications

Title deed

People who are famous or have been involved in a noteworthy undertaking sometimes choose to relay their stories in the form of an autobiography.

If you were to write a book about your life what would the title be? What main events would you want to include?

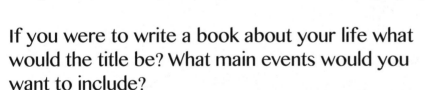

Stimulate Creative Thinking
© Will Hussey and Brilliant Publications

Life like?

Everybody's had one of those days that they'd perhaps rather forget. Sometimes events conspire to make you feel a little unhappy. For some people though, it has gotten a whole lot worse.

Recall and record all the 'worst days' in history: what happened and who experienced them?

Spitting image

When we think of friends and family, their appearance and personality combine to form an image of them in our mind.

Draw a caricature of yourself. Exaggerate your prominent features and try to capture something of the 'inside', as well as the outside.

Food for thought

Can you crack the code to work out what's on the menu?

Main courses

Side dishes/snacks

Desserts

Stimulate Creative Thinking
© Will Hussey and Brilliant Publications

Clothes label

If you think about your family and friends, they will probably be wearing particular favourite items of clothing you associate with them.

Write down items of clothing that are synonymous with people close to you. Find out if anyone else shares the same associations.

Slingshot

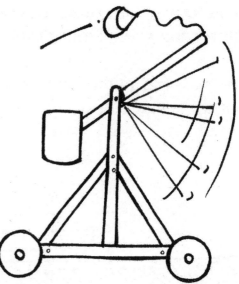

During the Middle Ages, a variety of weapons were used to attack an enemy: some for hand-to-hand contact and others to breach solid defences.

Design and make your own 'trebuchet', to hurl a ball of paper.

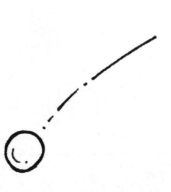

Think again

All of us can recall a situation when things didn't quite go to plan; hindsight is a wonderful thing.

What would you do differently if you had another opportunity? Explain what and why, and how the outcome might have been affected.

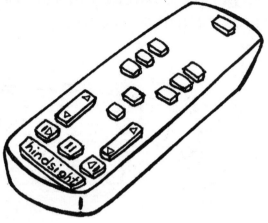

Stimulate Creative Thinking
© Will Hussey and Brilliant Publications

Up shot

Some days are just like any other days, until a chance encounter can lead to something exciting.

Write down a list of venues where something interesting seems more likely to occur.

For example, at the ice rink, on a railway platform, outside a stage door...

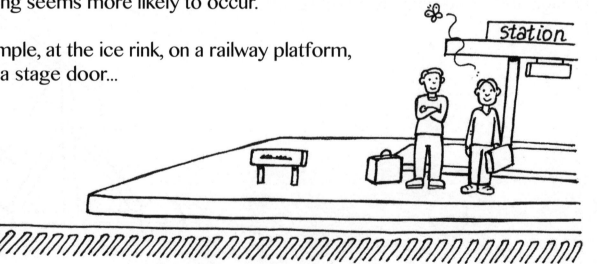

Stimulate Creative Thinking
© Will Hussey and Brilliant Publications

Nasty piece of work

Every superhero battles to overcome a nemesis – usually only just!

Devise and sketch your very own 'super villain' that will take some beating. What powers do they possess and dark deeds do they threaten?

Cross purposes

Planning ahead enables you to foresee any potential obstacles in your path. Some of these may seem easier to overcome than others.

Explain to someone which 'bridges you have left to cross' in order to achieve your goals. Do you have a strategy for success, or will you instead leave fate to take its course?

Watch stop

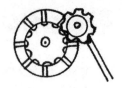

The inexorable march of time... We can't stop it, but we can measure it.

Devise and construct a device to gauge the passing of time. You can create your own 'units' of measurement, but try to make your timepiece as regular as clockwork!

Stimulate Creative Thinking
© Will Hussey and Brilliant Publications

Production line

Like it or not, supermarkets have become a weekly shopping fixture for many of us, offering an increasingly wide variety of items. How do we manage to locate what we need?

Recall and record all of the various signs that overhang the different aisles.

Stimulate Creative Thinking
© Will Hussey and Brilliant Publications

Take note

A kettledrum is not made from a kettle, and neither can you make music by blowing a shoehorn.

What alternative items could you use to produce musical notes and how? What names would you give to your musical instruments?

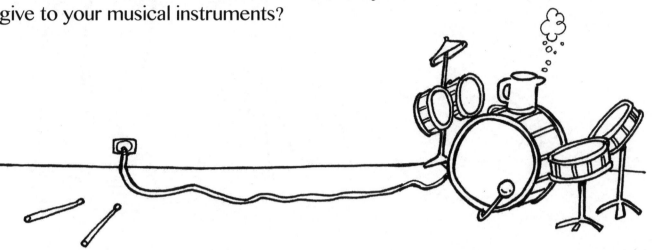

Aqu-attic

Fish are often associated with having very short memories, although the scientific evidence for this is inconclusive.

Plan and design an alternative fish tank that would prove to be simply unforgettable for its residents.

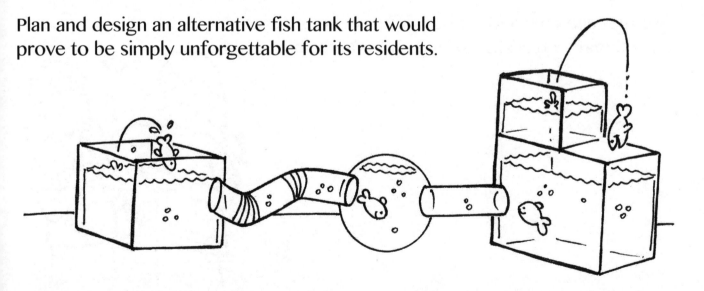

Fashion able?

Clothing trends come and go; the trick is to recognize what's 'in' at the moment.

Find a friend to debate 'what's hot' and what's not. Recommend an outfit to justify your selection.

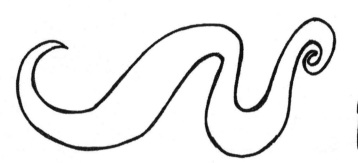 

Stimulate Creative Thinking

Sharp words

A film's special effects department is kept busy synthesizing a variety of different scenarios and conditions – including bumps and bruises.

Use masking tape and various different colours to try to create a realistic-looking cut or abrasion.

Stimulate Creative Thinking

Club together

Many children have interests and hobbies that they enjoy pursuing outside of school.

How many different clubs and organizations can you think of that exist in your locality? Generate a list of their names and the activities they provide.

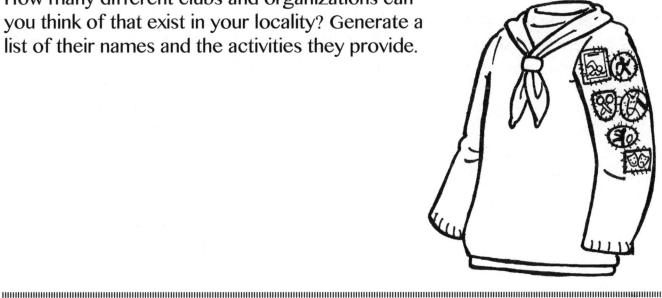

Drawing a blank

A 'light bulb moment' is when understanding finally dawns, and all becomes clear.

Recall and record all those times when you have remained completely bemused by a particular concept or explanation. Think of a term to describe such a lack of understanding: the opposite of a 'light bulb moment'.

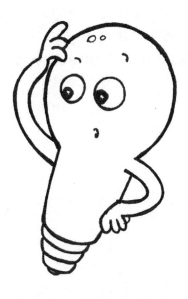

Cutting edge

A cheese grater cuts fairly uniform slithers of cheese – perhaps they could be a little more interesting.

Invent and illustrate a device that can cut and sculpt alternative shapes and sizes of cheese. Use labels and arrows to help indicate just how it works.

Stimulate Creative Thinking
© Will Hussey and Brilliant Publications

Like minded

Most people have a 'guilty pleasure' which they will only reluctantly admit to.

Try to discern some guilty pleasures of those people around you; consider what questions you can ask and how you can persuade them to divulge their likes!

Stimulate Creative Thinking
© Will Hussey and Brilliant Publications

Written transfer request

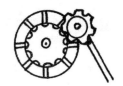

Isambard Kingdom Brunel is renowned for designing and building innovative bridges (amongst other things) during the Victorian era.

Carefully utilize card to create a bridging structure that will enable a marble to be transported from one side of a gap to the other.

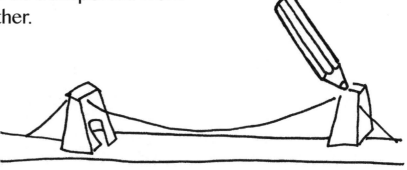

Flight log

'The world is your oyster...', perhaps even more so in recent years. Airplanes enable passengers to travel the globe in search of a chosen destination.

Investigate the furthest flight destinations available from your nearest airport. Decide whether to order them in terms of time taken or distance travelled. Which destinations can be flown to directly?

Earth works?

Some people would say that love makes the world go round, but others would argue that money is the most important.

Which do you think is true (if either) and why? Explain, in your opinion what the world requires to 'function' smoothly.

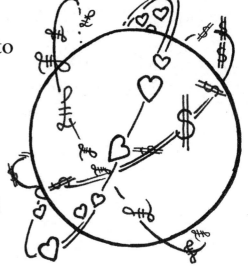

Stimulate Creative Thinking
© Will Hussey and Brilliant Publications

Cool uniform

The majority of school children in this country wear a designated school uniform; some of these outfits are perhaps more fashionable than others.

Design an alternative school uniform. Try to consider whether it is practical, as well as making it appeal to the majority. Would your uniform be appropriate for both pupils and teachers?

Stimulate Creative Thinking
© Will Hussey and Brilliant Publications

Food for thought

Can you crack the code to work out what's on the menu?

Main courses

Side dishes/snacks

Desserts

Four wheel strive

Vehicle registrations are unique, and can relay information regarding when and where that particular means of transport was constructed.

How many different vehicle registration plates can you memorize? Ask a friend to test you on your recall. Which of these vehicles is the oldest?

Stimulate Creative Thinking
© Will Hussey and Brilliant Publications

Set piece

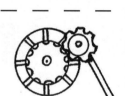

Some well-known board games will periodically change the counters they use for moving around the playing board. An 'iron' might be replaced by a 'guitar', for instance.

Design and construct a set of six new counters for a favourite board game; try to ensure there is a counter that would appeal to everyone.

Stimulate Creative Thinking
© Will Hussey and Brilliant Publications

Timely intervention

Not so long ago you would require a watch or a clock to help tell the time reasonably accurately. These days 'the time' is available on a wide range of different devices.

Identify and create a list of all the different items you come across that indicate the current time. For example, a cooker, phone, car dashboard...

Mixed messages

We all know of times when someone has said one thing and done the opposite.

Recall and record all the different examples of hypocrisy that you have encountered. Do you think the people involved were aware of their contradictions?

Pia know

The piano (or pianoforte) is one of the most popular instruments in the world. One of the first pianos is thought to have been built around the year 1700.

Try to sketch the keys of a piano. Label the different keys with appropriate musical notes if you can.

Stimulate Creative Thinking
© Will Hussey and Brilliant Publications

Present and correct?

Many people are fortunate to receive a variety of gifts for different occasions. Some of these presents are more memorable than others.

Catalogue all of the different items that you have received as presents. Record when you were given them and who they were from. Ask someone else to review your list – how do their recollections compare with yours?

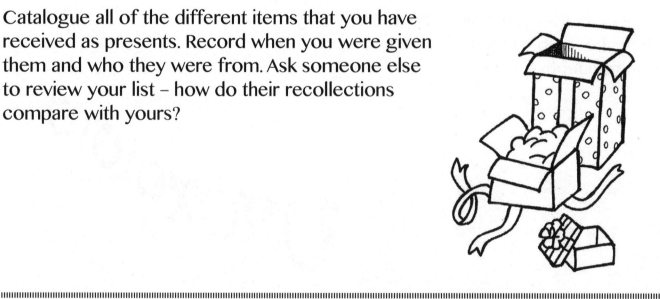

Stimulate Creative Thinking
© Will Hussey and Brilliant Publications

Fuss pot

When there is some sort of unnecessary commotion, you may hear the person responsible berated for 'making a fuss'.

Imagine what form a 'fuss' might take. Devise and construct a three-dimensional representation of your vision.

Brave art

Many of us have ambitious ideas and plans, yet for some reason we do not pursue them.

Compose a list of everything that you would like to do, if you knew you could not fail.

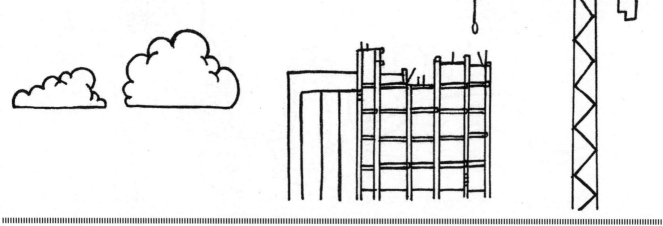
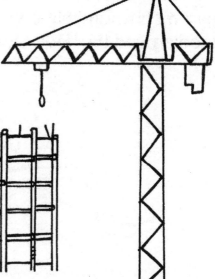

Jobs worth

Some jobs pay considerably more money than others, but perhaps this does not truly reflect the importance of certain roles in enabling society to function smoothly.

Of all the different types of jobs, which do you think are the most 'important' and why?

Stimulate Creative Thinking
© Will Hussey and Brilliant Publications

Pacemaker

Most of us can sketch a love heart, but what does a real heart look like?

Use your imagination to devise and draw a 'bionic' heart mechanism that could be used for pumping blood around the body. Don't forget to label it.

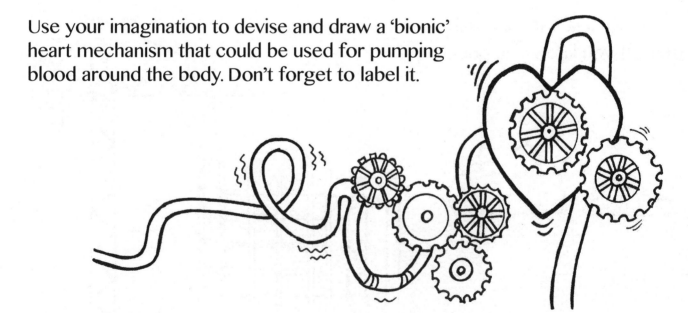

Stimulate Creative Thinking
© Will Hussey and Brilliant Publications

Accident log

We all know people who seem to have had more than their fair share of broken bones.

Conduct an informal survey between your friends and family to establish who is the most accident prone. Why do you think this might be?

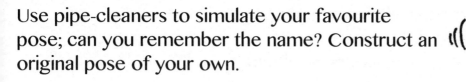

Yoga poser

Yoga exercises are thought to benefit both the mind and the body. Which is your favourite position?

Use pipe-cleaners to simulate your favourite pose; can you remember the name? Construct an original pose of your own.

Muscle definition

Depending on whom you ask, there are thought to be around 640 different muscles in the human body.

How many of these muscles can you name? Try to order them in size, from the largest to the smallest.

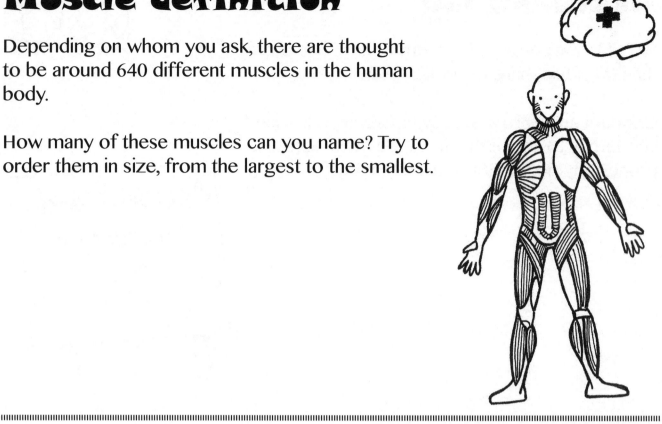

Stimulate Creative Thinking
© Will Hussey and Brilliant Publications

X, Y Q

Men and women have contrasting physical features, but perhaps there are also more subtle differences.

Apart from the obvious, record all the ways that you consider the genders to differ; you may choose to consider thoughts, behaviours, likes and dislikes.

Stimulate Creative Thinking
© Will Hussey and Brilliant Publications

Age difference

We are all subject to the process of ageing, although it is hard to detect from one day to the next.

Imagine your appearance years from now as you enter old age: sketch a portrait of yourself and consider the likely influence of family genetics.

Exchange rate

Most of us understand that 'appearances can be deceptive' and 'it's what's on the inside that counts'. That's not to say that we are all completely satisfied with our looks or mannerisms.

Which one thing would you change about yourself if you had the opportunity? Ask the same question to a friend and discuss the answer. Is their opinion the same?

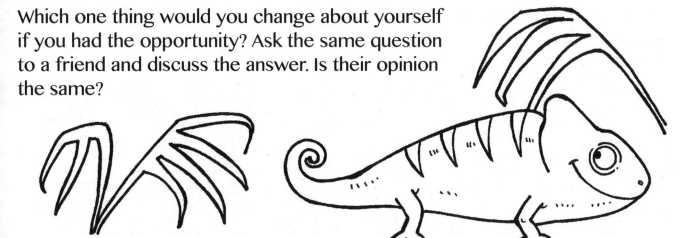

Propulsion compulsion

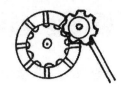

Toys are great. Toys that 'move' are even better!

Design and construct a device that can be propelled over a short distance. You could consider incorporating a wind-up mechanism, pulleys, magnets or maybe some other means.

Stimulate Creative Thinking
© Will Hussey and Brilliant Publications

Written prescription

There are drugs that can be good for you and those that are not.

Make a list of all the legal medicines that you can think of. Can you remember what they are for?

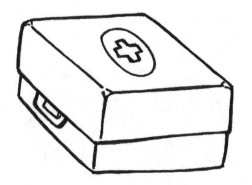

Stimulate Creative Thinking
© Will Hussey and Brilliant Publications

Ease yourself

Most of us don't like to boast, but there are some things that we are considerably better at than others.

Compose a list of all the things that you consider to be a 'piece of cake'. Justify your choices.

Tag line

Graffiti can range from simple written words to elaborate paintings and design. Sometimes artwork will reflect contemporary life.

Create a graffiti poster that conveys information about you; a pastiche of your life at this moment in time.

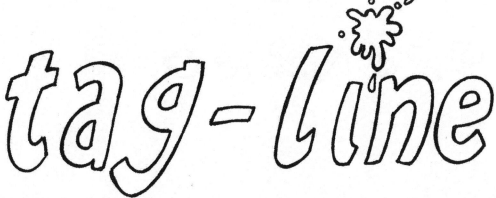

Food for thought

Can you crack the code to work out what's on the menu?

Main courses

Side dishes/snacks

Desserts

Stimulate Creative Thinking
© Will Hussey and Brilliant Publications

Wrist watch

Pulse rates can vary according to age, health and activity amongst other things.

Predict your own pulse rate before measuring it. How do the two readings compare? Do the same for the pulse rates of two other people; consider the factors that could affect their readings.

Italian job

Whilst most people like pizza, we vary greatly in our choice of preferred toppings.

Use junk materials to replicate your favourite pizza. How authentic can you make it look? Can anyone guess the 'flavour' of your favourite pizza?

Dogs differ

Dogs come in a huge variety in size and shapes, with appearances differing widely.

List all of the different breeds of dog that you can think of in height order. Which do you think are the most popular types?

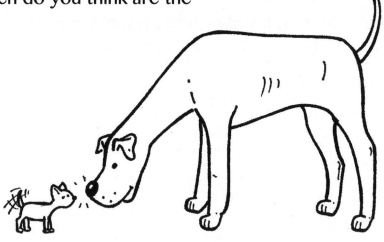

Stimulate Creative Thinking
© Will Hussey and Brilliant Publications

Suspended sentence

The idea of relaxing in a hammock on a warm summer's evening can be quite appealing. Finding suitable anchors to secure the hammock can be more of a challenge.

Consider all of the places you know of that might be suitable to suspend your hammock. Which is your preferred location?

Stimulate Creative Thinking
© Will Hussey and Brilliant Publications

Bureau de change

School desks have evolved over the years; from the wooden hinged-top variety with inkwells to simple plastic tables.

Invent and design an 'integrated' workplace that would be of real use to you: consider everything you might need in today's hi-tech world.

Twisted meaning

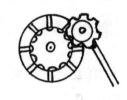

Whilst a paper clip is a useful piece of office equipment, it can also be tempting to re-form.

Analyse your day so far: choose a word that best reflects your current mood and bend paper clips to represent the letters. Ask someone to try to decipher your word.

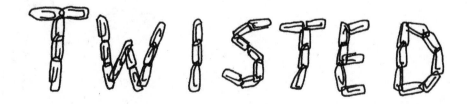

Key moment

A key ring is perhaps a way of personalizing a set of keys; making something functional individual to our own particular taste.

Create and make a key ring that reflects your personal characteristics. Try to ensure your design is both simple yet effective.

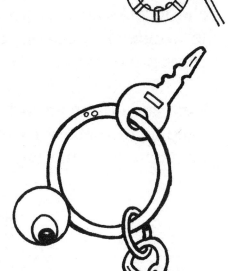

Stimulate Creative Thinking
© Will Hussey and Brilliant Publications

Song title

Songs can be about special times or places – and often people.

Think of all the songs that contain the name of a person in the lyrics. Devise a list of the songs and the people they refer to.

Stimulate Creative Thinking
© Will Hussey and Brilliant Publications

Waiting gain

Although time continues to pass, the way we choose to measure it can vary.

Imagine there were actually twenty-four months in a year. Consider what the possible consequences might be; do the advantages outweigh the disadvantages?

Moving arts

An internal combustion engine generates the energy required to propel a vehicle – but just what does one look like?

Sketch what you envisage an engine looks like underneath the bonnet. Can you name any of the components?

Hot spot

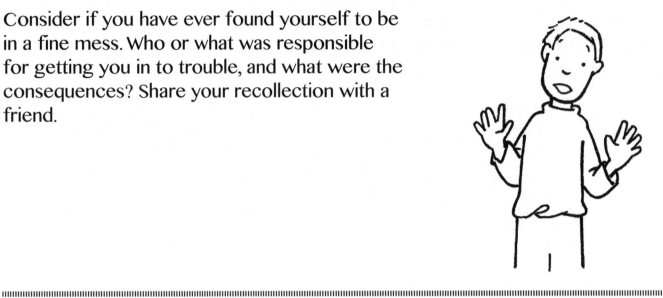

When events conspire to place someone in an unpleasant predicament, it can sometimes be referred to as a 'fine mess'.

Consider if you have ever found yourself to be in a fine mess. Who or what was responsible for getting you in to trouble, and what were the consequences? Share your recollection with a friend.

Stimulate Creative Thinking
© Will Hussey and Brilliant Publications

Knows piece

Scents make cents: perfumes and aftershaves are big business, with new brands making their way on to the shop shelves every week.

Devise a box for packaging a new scent to be launched. Carefully consider the name of your product, and how it will appeal to customers.

Stimulate Creative Thinking
© Will Hussey and Brilliant Publications

Better judgement

Whilst most of us would probably prefer not to require medical treatment, the majority of the population has visited hospital at least once in their lives.

Generate a list of everything you are likely to find in a hospital building.

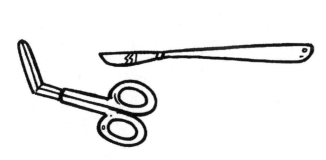

Trivial pursuit

We can all remember some things better than others – usually significant events and encounters are the easiest to recall.

Which trivial events can you recall in your life? How long ago did they occur and why do you think they have remained in your memory?

Road work

Traffic signs inform and advise road users about avoiding potential hazards and ensuring a safe journey.

Alternatively, imagine if traffic signs were intended to encourage you to reach your destination in the shortest possible time: what would they look like and what messages would they impart? Sketch your ideas.

Stimulate Creative Thinking
© Will Hussey and Brilliant Publications

Cross words

Everybody experiences 'ups and downs' and sometimes those least enjoyable moments manifest into an argument or disagreement of some sort.

What do people 'usually' argue about? Are there any common causes of conflict, and how are they typically resolved? Design a questionnaire and research the views and opinions of several friends or family members.

Stimulate Creative Thinking
© Will Hussey and Brilliant Publications

Flight plan

Most paper planes manage to complete at least a short flight – influencing their direction is considerably trickier.

Design and build a stunt paper aeroplane that will successfully incorporate a 'loop-the-loop' into its flight.

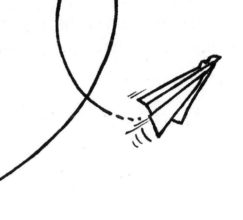

Trees company

Even in cities, we are never too far away from a tree; they provide homes for wildlife, clean the air and enhance the look of an area.

But how much notice do we take of these ever-present woody neighbours? Can you complete a map that includes every single tree in your local area? Can you identify any particular species of trees?

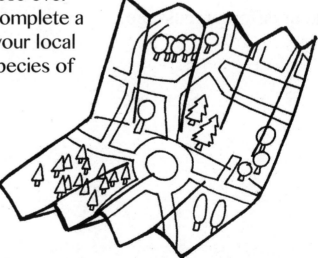

Still determined

We have various characteristics that help to define our personality. Certain objects can also be described in similar fashion: a chest of drawers might be described as being 'regal' or a comfortable pair of boots as being 'trusty'.

If your friends and family were portrayed as inanimate objects, then what would they be and why?

Stimulate Creative Thinking
© Will Hussey and Brilliant Publications

Brand new?

A logo is a design that represents an organization: most large companies have easily recognizable logos.

Can you adapt a well-known logo to portray a quite different message?

Stimulate Creative Thinking
© Will Hussey and Brilliant Publications

Familiar faces

A euphemism is an expression used in place of a more literal meaning; having 'forty winks' means to take a short nap, for instance.

List all of the different euphemisms you can think of. Ask a friend if they can decipher the meanings.

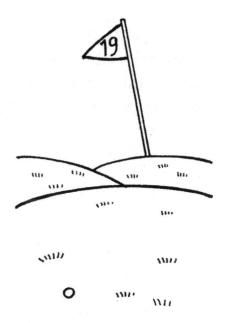

Making headway

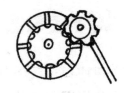

Athletes sometimes choose to wear headbands as part of their attire, either for practical reasons, or simply as a fashion accessory.

Create and make a stylish headband that conveys your personal preferences: hobbies, colours, music and anything else you would like to incorporate in to the design.

Animal instinct

The 'philosophant' is a fictional name used to describe a 'philosophical elephant'.

Consider how to blend the names of other animals with descriptive terms to create fictional new creatures. Can anyone work out which combinations you have used?

Stimulate Creative Thinking
© Will Hussey and Brilliant Publications

Write move?

Some things are just plainly 'wrong': events, sayings, occurrences or combinations that seem unpleasant to contemplate.

Record some examples of 'poor taste' that you would prefer not to experience.

For example, sandals worn over socks, passive smoking, mouldy bread...

Stimulate Creative Thinking
© Will Hussey and Brilliant Publications

Forward thinking

Humans have evolved over millions of years into their current form.

Imagine how we might evolve in another few million years; sketch your vision.

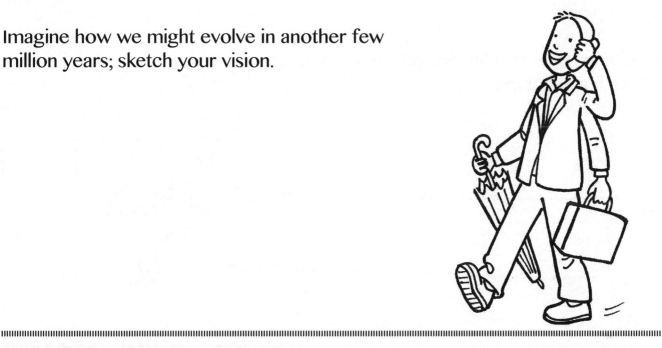

Love letters

How many different songs can you think of containing the word 'love' in their title?

Compose a list and see if a friend can make any additional contributions.

Drainwave

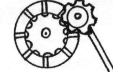

Something that flashes by particularly quickly and suddenly can be compared to moving 'like a rat up a drainpipe'.

Devise and create a life-like rat for squeezing through a drainpipe.

Stimulate Creative Thinking
© Will Hussey and Brilliant Publications

Bone structure

Your ankle bone is connected to the leg bone, your leg bone's connected to the knee bone... The medical profession uses rather more technical terms to name the bones of the body.

Construct a labelled diagram of the human skeleton, using as many scientific names for the various bones as you can think of.

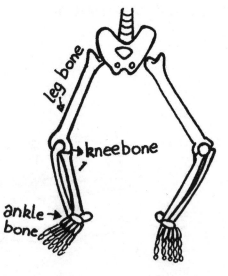

Stimulate Creative Thinking
© Will Hussey and Brilliant Publications

Food for thought

Can you crack the code to work out what's on the menu?

Main courses

Side dishes/snacks

Desserts

Creature feature

The Olympic games is perhaps the ultimate goal for sportsmen and women across a wide range of disciplines.

Imagine animals could compete alongside humans; which sports might the various species excel at?

Stimulate Creative Thinking
© Will Hussey and Brilliant Publications

Base line

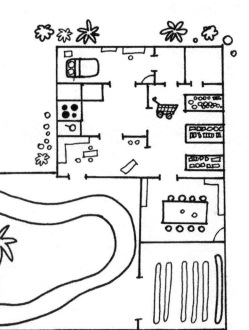

Imagine you were building a luxury mansion and could afford to include everything you desired.

Create a floor plan for your new home. What features would you include? Annotate your plan.

Stimulate Creative Thinking
© Will Hussey and Brilliant Publications

Isle of wonder

Consider which three things you would take with you if you were to live on an isolated desert island.

Compare your choices with those of a friend: can you convince them of the validity of your own selection?

String section

Artists sometimes utilize a variety of unusual media to create their masterpieces.

Coil string on to card to create a picture of a favourite animal; can anyone correctly identify your chosen subject?

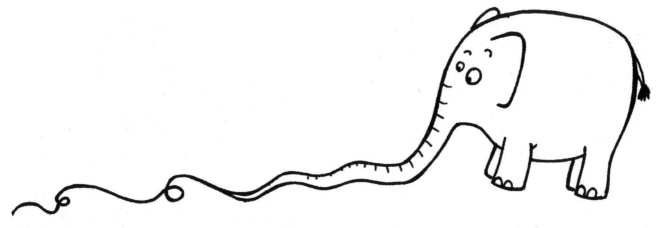

Breathe easy?

It's estimated that school children take between twenty and thirty breaths each minute.

Consider everything you could do in the space of a single breath; make a list of your favourite suggestions

For example, text LOL to my friend, complete a cartwheel, make a sandcastle...

Stimulate Creative Thinking
© Will Hussey and Brilliant Publications

Sleight of hand

We all know that 'honesty is the best policy', although there are perhaps some exceptions to the rule.

Explain which 'white lies' are commonly thought to be acceptable. Do you agree?

Stimulate Creative Thinking
© Will Hussey and Brilliant Publications

Written off

A shopping list is perhaps a way of ensuring the kitchen cupboard is fully stocked for the week – that's assuming that everything's included on the list...

List those items that always seem to be omitted; do you think there is a reason for this?

Dream liner

Whilst there are many dreams that we are unable to remember, some are more vivid and easier to recollect.

Illustrate a scene from a particularly memorable dream. Can you decipher any underlying 'meaning' associated with your vision?

Back story

Choose a close friend or family member.
Compose a blurb for a biography of their life,
omitting the name.

Share your paragraph with others: can they
recognize who the subject of your writing is?
Would they make any significant changes?

Stimulate Creative Thinking
© Will Hussey and Brilliant Publications

Flights of fancy

A dart's 'flight' is intended to stabilize it, enabling a
smoother trajectory towards the board.

Design and make your own personalized flights
for a set of darts.

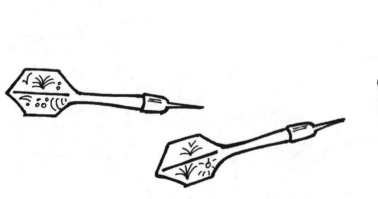

Stimulate Creative Thinking
© Will Hussey and Brilliant Publications

Sound judgement

Noises range from excruciatingly loud to imperceptibly quiet; fortunately most fall somewhere between the two extremes.

Rank the volume levels that you have been exposed to, from loudest to quietest. Describe the source of the sound; were some more bearable than others?

Under hand

In an ideal world fair play, endeavour and ability would surely be rewarded.

Do cheats ever prosper? Can you think of any instances when dishonest tactics, lying or cheating have been rewarded?

Ink well?

Body art is becoming increasingly popular, with
people expressing a wide variety of pictures,
words and patterns by using their skin as a canvas.

A tattoo is a permanent fixture: sketch a design
that you might regret having done in later years.

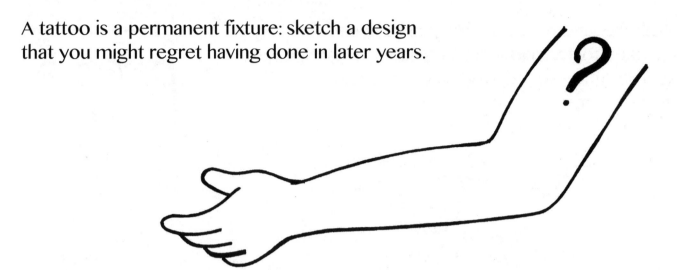

Stimulate Creative Thinking
© Will Hussey and Brilliant Publications

Flicks chart

Everyone has a shortlist of favourite films,
although we have all endured movies that remain
in the memory for the wrong reasons.

Conduct a straw poll of friends and family to
determine the most unpopular films: do they have
anything in common? Is there a way to ensure the
same mistake is not repeated?

Stimulate Creative Thinking
© Will Hussey and Brilliant Publications

Double vision

Three-dimensional printers are beginning to reproduce items ranging from car parts to dolls' houses.

Choose a three-dimensional object and using card, try to replicate it as closely as you can. Evaluate your attempt when you have completed it: what could you do differently next time?

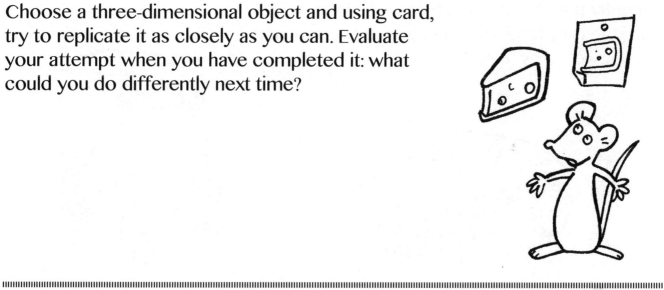

Written off

There is sometimes talk of how great life used to be in 'the good old days'. Of course, things often appear rosier with a little hindsight.

What was it like in 'the bad old days'? Consider how things have changed for the better and list some comparisons.

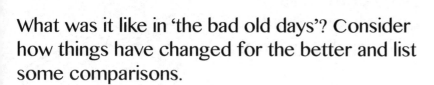

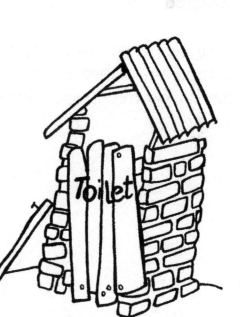

Carriage clocked

Horse and carts preceded motorcars as a method of public transport.

Consider a motorized vehicle that you have recently travelled in; sketch how an 'equivalent' carriage may have looked in days gone by when it was powered by horses.

Stimulate Creative Thinking

Written constitution

It is amazing what you can sometimes find wedged down the back or sides of a settee.

Imagine the queen's servants have not been as scrupulous in their duties as they perhaps should have: what might you find down the back of a royal sofa?

Stimulate Creative Thinking

Seamless transition

Ask several people to write 'half' a sentence, leaving the pen they used with you.

Complete the sentences, trying to ensure that the handwriting and content matches the sample provided. Share your efforts: can the original authors identify the point where you continued their writing?

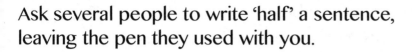

Ask several people to write 'half'...

Make believe

Some years ago two young girls fooled the world in to thinking there really were fairies at the bottom of their garden, by making cardboard drawings and photographing them.

Create a magical creature of some sort and photograph it in a particular habitat. How realistic can you make the scene look?

Lost forewords

Many people possess more books than can be squeezed on to their bookshelves; they become prized and cherished possessions.

Try to catalogue every book that you own from memory: it is unusual to recall more than half!

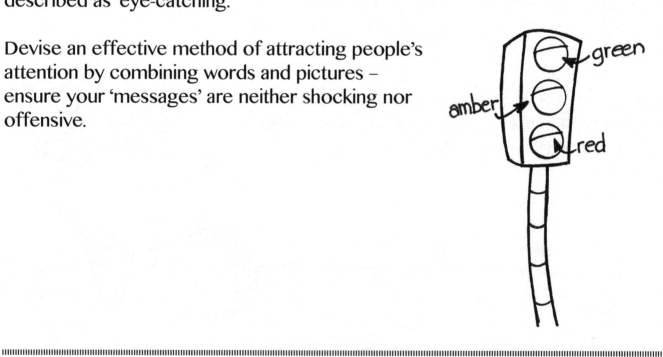

Stimulate Creative Thinking
© Will Hussey and Brilliant Publications

Watchword

A design is sometimes complimented by being described as 'eye-catching.'

Devise an effective method of attracting people's attention by combining words and pictures – ensure your 'messages' are neither shocking nor offensive.

Stimulate Creative Thinking
© Will Hussey and Brilliant Publications

Food for thought

Can you crack the code to work out what's on the menu?

Main courses

Side dishes/snacks

Desserts

Danger money

Some professions are considered more hazardous than others: either because there is a significant risk of serious injury or relatively minor mishaps are commonplace.

Of all the different occupations you can think of, which would you describe as a 'risky business'?

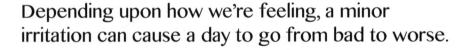

Stimulate Creative Thinking
© Will Hussey and Brilliant Publications

Rash decision

Depending upon how we're feeling, a minor irritation can cause a day to go from bad to worse.

Identify those relatively small incidents that can disproportionately affect your mood. For example, forgetting to charge your phone, recording the wrong TV programme, dropping your last sweet on to the pavement...

Stimulate Creative Thinking
© Will Hussey and Brilliant Publications

Recorded delivery

According to the Christmas nativity story, gifts included gold, frankincense and myrrh.

What three modern-day alternatives could be presented to an extremely important guest?

Stimulate Creative Thinking
© Will Hussey and Brilliant Publications

Positive thinking

Whilst most of us have a few regrets, conversely we also have memories and achievements worth celebrating.

Make a list of everything about your life that makes you feel proud.

Stimulate Creative Thinking
© Will Hussey and Brilliant Publications

Fe line

It is said that a cat has nine lives.

Draw alternative ways that a cat might meet its demise.

Stimulate Creative Thinking

Star track

In today's society, social networking enables many people to access a mass audience.

Who do you think are the three most famous people on the planet? Why? Ask the same question of a friend and debate your responses.

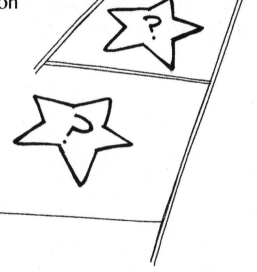

Stimulate Creative Thinking

Quantitative easy?

The US dollar is the most commonly traded currency on the planet, ahead of the euro and the Japanese yen.

Create and make your own monetary currency; consider designing a combination of notes and coins.

End game

A novel must have a satisfying conclusion that proves agreeable to the reader.

Recall and record as many conclusions to books you have read as possible. Which were particularly memorable and why?

Under ground

We are encouraged to pick up items that have mistakenly been knocked to the floor, but is there really any harm to be done?

Predict those items around your house that would be crushed if someone trod on them. Create a 'crush list'.

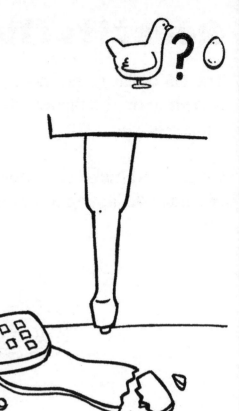

Stimulate Creative Thinking
© Will Hussey and Brilliant Publications

Drawing to a conclusion

Recall some of the memorable conclusions to books you have read.

Select a favourite 'ending' and transform it into a picture that conveys the scene as effectively as you can.

Stimulate Creative Thinking
© Will Hussey and Brilliant Publications

Repeat prescription

Teachers are renowned for repeating certain words and phrases.

Investigate the most common classroom catchphrases: gather the opinions of friends and family to ascertain the top three.

For example, 'that bell is for me, not for you...'

Art work

Sculptures are sometimes used to add an interesting dimension to a relatively plain area of land.

Design a three-dimensional piece of artwork to transform a suitable location. What will you create and where will you position it? Try to think of a design that is sympathetic to the surroundings.

Chip shot

Crisps remain a popular snack with an ever-increasing array of variety and flavours on offer.

Research and record all the different variations of crisps that are available. Categorize those that are relatively new flavours and the more traditional favourites.

Stimulate Creative Thinking

Written down

Sometimes we all get what can be described as a 'sinking feeling' when anticipating something we are not looking forward to.

What gives you that sinking feeling? Explain why you think this happens in certain situations.

Stimulate Creative Thinking

Inside story

The human body has a variety of internal organs that help us to function effectively.

How many of these different organs can you find out about? Try to draw each one and write down their purpose.

Lesson plan

Children spend over 180 days a year attending school – that's a lot of lesson time.

What activities would you like to add to or remove from the school timetable? Design a questionnaire to gather information from some of your friends before constructing an alternative timetable.

Tree hows

Just as experts can analyse handwriting to provide clues about someone's personality, sketching a tree can hint at similar traits.

Create and make a tree that conveys something of your appearance and personality.

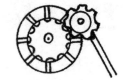

Stimulate Creative Thinking
© Will Hussey and Brilliant Publications

Fence post

Most people have been faced with a dilemma at some point in their lives.

Make a flow chart to show the different thought processes that enabled you to arrive at a difficult decision.

Stimulate Creative Thinking
© Will Hussey and Brilliant Publications

A question of sport

Sports and games are popular pursuits for millions of people across the globe; some have evolved over centuries whilst other activities are relatively new.

Devise your own original game: prepare a set of rules and remember to think of a suitable title.

Cocoa means

Many people share a liking for chocolate; a vast array of confectionary, biscuits and cakes share the magic ingredient.

Plan and design your own chocolate factory. Consider what is processed and how this might be achieved; include labels to clarify any important procedures.

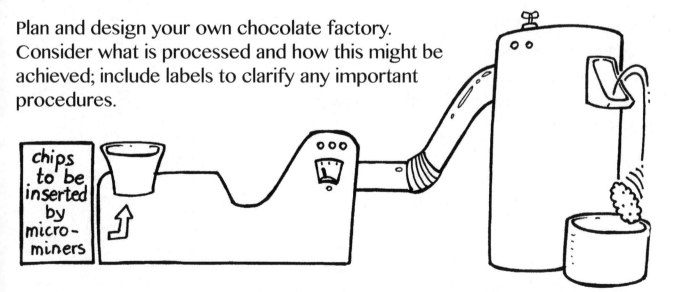

chips to be inserted by micro-miners

Age concern

If you could immediately be any age you desired, how old would you choose to be?

Design a questionnaire to elicit the answer to this question: do the responses vary significantly according to the age of the people you ask?

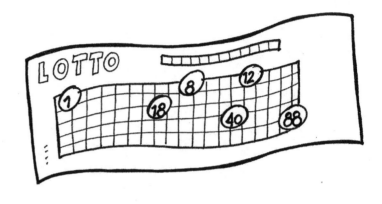

Stimulate Creative Thinking
© Will Hussey and Brilliant Publications

Hang time

Many children and adults enjoy the challenge of adventurous activities such as rock climbing, canoeing and waterskiing.

Construct a model of a climbing frame that would appeal to all your friends and family. You can include swings, slides and any other mechanism that might provide suitable challenge and enjoyment.

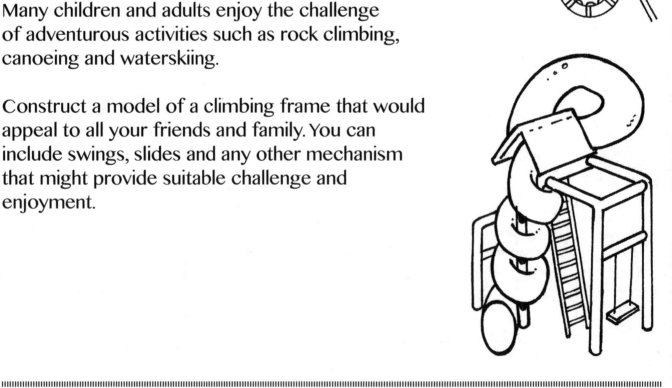

Stimulate Creative Thinking
© Will Hussey and Brilliant Publications

Light touch

Photographic images taken from space reveal the extent of light created from many different sources.

Prepare a list of everything on earth that illuminates, from just a tiny glow to dazzling brilliance.

Planet rock

Whilst it may be a nice idea, sadly we know that the moon is not actually made from cheese.

But imagine it was: create a solar system consisting entirely of food. What would the planets be called, and what would they be made of?

Food for thought

Can you crack the code to work out what's on the menu?

Main courses

Side dishes/snacks

Desserts

Stimulate Creative Thinking

Cats or dogs?

Some people are definitely dog lovers whilst others prefer cats as pets. Both animals have endearing features.

Construct a chart to compare which of the two animals makes the best pet: list all their various attributes to arrive at a definitive answer.

Amazing space

Most of us become used to a familiar routine that we follow from one day to the next.

Occasionally we encounter an unexpected happening or event, which elevates our day from the mundane to extraordinary, such as waking up to unexpected fresh blanket of snow or a duck waddling into your classroom!

Select a particularly brilliant thing that has happened to you and construct a jigsaw puzzle to represent it. Some pieces of the puzzle will be probably be rather boring and ordinary – but what will be on the extraordinary ones?

Head room

The human brain has been described as the world's most powerful computer.

Design and build a three-dimensional interpretation of the brain, using mechanical components to portray your 'super computer'.

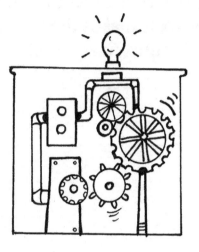

Stimulate Creative Thinking
© Will Hussey and Brilliant Publications

Under write

It takes a special type of person to be a successful spy, requiring particular qualities to complete covert missions.

Complete a school report for a potential spy. Consider the characteristics a teacher might perceive to be strengths and weaknesses.

Stimulate Creative Thinking
© Will Hussey and Brilliant Publications

Grill seeker

It is not only when buying a house that 'location' is considered to be very important.

Imagine you sold burgers for a living: where might be the ideal places to position your van in order to sell the most burgers?

Water way

The saying 'like a fish out of water' can apply to somebody attempting to complete an unfamiliar task.

If you've ever owned a goldfish you probably know how difficult they can be to transport. Devise and sketch some alternative ways of taking your goldfish on holiday.

Pop the question

Popcorn is a popular treat when viewing a movie. The kernels usually require heating in order to make them 'pop'.

Make a list of alternative ways of preparing your popcorn: how many innovative ways can you think of for popping your popcorn?

Stimulate Creative Thinking
© Will Hussey and Brilliant Publications

Ageing process

They say that 'you can't teach an old dog new tricks' – but maybe that's not necessarily so.

Ask an older friend or family member for assistance: can you coach them into learning a 'new' skill that they are unfamiliar with?

Stimulate Creative Thinking
© Will Hussey and Brilliant Publications

Letters of the law

Some countries of the world are governed by
what could be described as a 'dictatorship'; the
population are told what to do and have little say in
deciding the rules and laws of the land.

Write a constitution for your own dictatorship.
What rules would you enforce and which laws
would you pass?

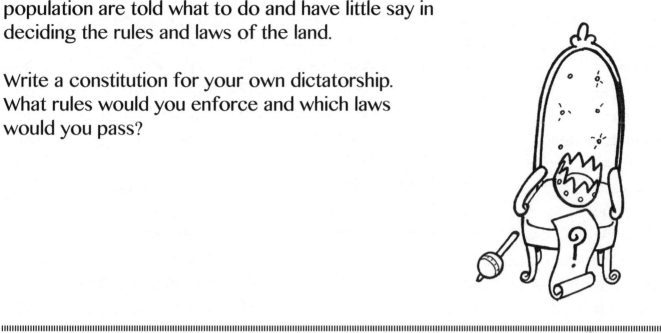

Reward chart

Whether it's eating a meal, or relaxing at the end
of a busy day, children and adults alike will often
reward themselves by saving the 'best 'till last.'

Consider your friends and family: what sort of
things do they reward themselves for and what
with?

Index

Food for thought - answer sheet

Page 21
Main courses
Americana pizza
Corned beef hash

Side dishes/snacks
Caesar salad
French fries

Desserts
Knickerbocker glory
Mississippi mud pie

Page 32
Main courses
Lasagne
Pasta carbonara

Side dishes/snacks
Minestrone soup
Cornish pasty

Desserts
Semolina
Lemon sorbet

Page 43
Main courses
Beef bourguinon
Moussaka

Side dishes/snacks
Yorkshire pudding
Ciabatta

Desserts
Ice cream
Banoffee pie

Page 54
Main courses
Cumberland sausages
Haggis

Side dishes/snacks
Black pudding
Macaroni cheese

Desserts
Bakewell tart
Rhubarb crumble

Page 69
Main courses
Chicken fajitas
Lancashire hot pot

Side dishes/snacks
Bombay mix
Poppadoms

Desserts
Rice pudding
Victoria sponge

Page 81
Main courses
Bangers and mash
Shepherd's pie

Side dishes/snacks
Toad in the hole
Welsh rarebit

Desserts
Hot cross buns
Blancmange

Page 94
Main courses
Spaghetti bolognese
Risotto

Side dishes/snacks
Spanish omelette
Sushi

Desserts
Spotted dick
Raspberry pavlova

a	b	c	d	e
🍎	🍌		🥕	
f	g	h	i	j
🐟				
k	l	m	n	o
p	r	s	t	u
v	w	x	y	z

Lightning Source UK Ltd.
Milton Keynes UK
UKOC01f1947271014

240654UK00009B/30/P